PREACHING TO THE CONVERTED

Peter Porter

PREACHING TO THE CONVERTED

LONDON
OXFORD UNIVERSITY PRESS
1972

Oxford University Press, Ely House, London W.1

GLASGOW NEW YORK TORONTO MELBOURNE WELLINGTON
CAPE TOWN IBADAN NAIROBI DAR ES SALAAM LUSAKA ADDIS ABABA
DELHI BOMBAY CALCUTTA MADRAS KARACHI LAHORE DACCA
KUALA LUMPUR SINGAPORE HONG KONG TOKYO

ISBN 0 19 211821 8

© *Oxford University Press* 1972

PRINTED IN GREAT BRITAIN
BY THE BOWERING PRESS PLYMOUTH

For Jannice and for Jane

CONTENTS

ACKNOWLEDGEMENTS

ACKNOWLEDGEMENTS are due to the editors of the following periodicals in which some of these poems first appeared: *Ambit, The Carleton Miscellany, The Consort, Encounter, The Listener, London Magazine, New Statesman, Outposts, Overland, Poets' Choice*, 1971 (*Island Press, Sydney*), *Poetry Book Society Christmas Supplement*, 1970, *The Review, Second Aeon, Times Literary Supplement, Tracks, Transatlantic Review*, and *Wave*. One poem was a *Leeds New Poets Broadsheet*, and another was first heard over the *London Poetry Secretariat's Dial-a-Poem Service*. Acknowledgements are also due to the *BBC* in whose programmes some other poems were first read.

THE OLD ENEMY

God is a Super-Director
who's terribly good at crowd scenes,
but He has only one tense, the present.
Think of pictures—
Florentine or Flemish, with Christ
or a saint—the softnesses of Luke,
skulls of Golgotha, craftsmen's
instruments of torture—everything is go!
Angels are lent for the moment,
villains and devils are buying Hell
on HP, pain is making faces.
In the calmer sort of painting,
serenely kneeling, since they paid for it,
the donor and his family keep the clocking now.
They say, Lord, we know
Lazarus is king in Heaven
but here in Prato it would be death to trade:
the death of God requires a merchant's dignity
and so they tip their fingers in an arch
that runs from Christ's erection
to a *Landsknecht* leaning on his arquebus.
Those centuries were twice the men
that MGM are—God loves music
and architecture, pain and palm trees,
anything to get away from time.

THE KING OF THE CATS IS DEAD

The light on his thigh was like
a waterfall in Iceland, and his hair
was the tidal rip between two rocks,
his claws retracted sat in softness
deeper than the ancient moss of Blarney,
his claws extended were the coulter
of the gods and a raw March wind
was in his merely agricultural yawn.
Between his back legs was a catapult
of fecundity and he was riggish
as a red-haired man. The girls
of our nation felt him brush their legs
when they were bored with telling rosaries—
at night he clawed their brains in their
coffined beds and his walnut mind
wrinkled on their scalps. His holidays
were upside down in water and then
his face was like the sun: his smell
was in the peat smoke and even his midden
was a harmony of honey. When he stalked
his momentary mice the land shook
as though Atlantic waves were bowling
at the western walls. But his eyes
were the greatest thing about him.
They burned low and red so that drunks
saw them like two stars above a hedge,
they held the look of last eyes
in a drowning man, they were the sight
the rebel angels saw the first morning
of expulsion. And he is dead—a voice
from the centre of the earth told of his death
by treachery, that he lies in a hole
of infamy, his kidneys and his liver
torn from his body.

                    Therefore tell
the men and horses of the marketplace,
the swallows laying twigs, the salmon
on the ladder that nothing is
as it has been
                    time is explored
and all is known, the portents
are of brief and brutal things, since
all must hear the words of desolation,
The King of the Cats is Dead
                    and it
is only Monday in the world.

PREACHING TO THE CONVERTED

Calling down the funnel of your mind
News the charnel chords make *larmoyant*,
The Pretenders come, of black and silver face—
The Old is painted on an eye, he's Sleep,
The shadow of a never-noticed death,
The New is pictured on a box, he dreams
Of Ever-Afternoon, Ego-Eternity:
Great Abstracts, which our thin vocabulary
Strains to make real: and this is poetry.

Strung down the classic nave of San Lorenzo,
Gouty and gorgeous as the flesh puts on,
Howls of the damned, the stretched-out cries of love,
Heard all before and when the wind blows heard
Over water to the Marble Island: never
Like Mother or the Moon to rise in state
Casting their grave clothes, no territorial
Imperative remaining—only to huddle close
Under the sermon shower: God will be verbose.

Preaching to the Converted is preaching Time,
The only subject that memorials hear;
They wink their Latin letters, listen at angles
To rhetoric till their sculpted knees are knocking—
This is the height God's words have risen to,
Beyond it you are free—you poet, you philosopher,
You driver on the autobahn—the base is fixed:
A *Grundrisse* for the dead—have marble fun,
Put on your shoes and walk into the sun.

TIMOR MORTIS

As Schopenhauer's coach rolls
the worms in the panelling
start a schottische—

Sister and brother in the mitral dark,
when we go we are single,
our hanclasp's broken—

But clocks are still clocking,
strangers are dreaming
identical dreams—

Hailed out of nothing and with
nowhere to go but a spread
sail of theory. Ever and ever—

We would escape if
the raft could hold all of us:
I'm in the painting—

Touch is the touch paper,
the fuse in the tail,
the sermon in silver—

The plague town behind him,
relaxed with a nosegay,
Schopenhauer mutters—

Man is ridiculous; if
it weren't for his death,
he'd have no value whatever—

FOSSIL GATHERING

Armed with hammers, we move along the cliff
Whose blue wall keeps a million million deaths;
The surf is low, the heat haze screens the stiff-
Backed searchers for imprisoned crystals. Blind
Eyes of belemnites watch from narrow clefts,
Jurassic sun shines on them while they're mined.

The children look them up in paperbacks
And break an Ancient with impatient ease.
Sorted and cleaned, the fossils are in stacks,
Prepared and dressed for classrooms and jam jars—
At night in cupboards the re-assembled seas
Break over England, straining for the stars.

A Little Guide in Colour tells us how
These creatures sank in their unconscious time,
That life in going leaves a husk the plough
Or amateur collector can displace,
That every feeling thing ascends from slime
To selfhood and in dying finds a face.

MAY, 1945

As the Allied tanks trod Germany to shard
and no man had seen a fresh-pressed uniform
for six months, as the fire storm
bit out the core of Dresden yard by yard,

as farmers hid turnips for the after-war,
as cadets going to die passed Waffen SS
tearing identifications from their battledress,
the Russians only three days from the Brandenburger Tor—

in the very hell of sticks and blood and brick dust
as Germany the phoenix burned, the wraith
of History pursed its lips and spoke, thus:

To go with teeth and toes and human soap,
the radio will broadcast Bruckner's Eighth
so that good and evil may die in equal hope.

EVOLUTION
For D. J. Enright

From Minneapolis and Rio, from Sydney and Hendon South,
    they will tunnel through the soil
  (old mole in *Hamlet* and the kids' cartoons)
    and eventually they'll end up here.
This is the Jewish Cemetery at the foot of
    The Mount of Olives. From my point of view
  (and I have been calling myself a residual Christian),
    a cemetery without crosses and headstones
looks like a stonemason's junkyard. But
    just beyond the cemetery is the Garden
of Gethsemane, the Vale of Kidron, the Dome
    of the Rock, and the Eastern Wall
with its Gate for the Messiah to come through
    (decently bricked-up). Staring in sunlight,
I am conscious only of the Jewish Resurrection—
    Christians can resurrect anywhere,
but every Jew has to go by underground:
    out of Cracow or Lodz, with his diary's
death, from the musical comedy stage of
    New York, from the pages of fiery
Medieval books—he dives into oblivion
    and comes up here to join the queues
as the millions swapping stories enter Heaven.
    How hot and dirty and pale are olive leaves,
how one's heart beats above the golden city,
    which really belongs to architects,
archaeologists, and such Sunday Schools as we have left.
    None of it's as real as a carved camel
or a smudgy glass ring, except this Resurrection:
    I can see this easily, and if the boys
flogging panoramic views would just keep quiet
    I could hear the first tapping on a plate.
Now we are changed: I haven't an atom

in my body which I brought to Europe
in 1951. How beautiful is evolution,
    that I am moving deeper into my own brain.
The air is filled with something
    and I will not call it light—
stay with me, my friends; truth and love,
like miracles, need nowhere at all to happen in.

SEX AND THE OVER FORTIES

It's too good for them,
they look so unattractive undressed—
let them read paperbacks!

A few things to keep in readiness—
a flensing knife, a ceiling mirror,
a cassette of *The Broken Heart*.

More luncheons than lust,
more meetings on Northern Line stations,
more discussions of children's careers.

A postcard from years back—
I'm twenty-one, in Italy and in love!
Wagner wrote *Tristan* at forty-four.

Trying it with noises and in strange positions,
trying it with the young themselves,
trying to keep it up with the Joneses!

All words and no play,
all animals fleeing a forest fire,
all Apollo's grafters running.

Back to the dream in the garden,
back to the pictures in the drawer,
back to back, tonight and every night.

NOTES TO A BIOGRAPHER

I've only sailed through the Mediterranean—
eight hours in Naples, three stops
at Port Said; I didn't even get off the ship
last time at Gib—
I've never been on Ulysses' island
or on Isherwood's
or skin-dived with Swedes
and galley-slaves off Lindos—
if then a Prince would pay for it
my *Italienische Reise* is ready to go—
let the mad Cambridge cyclist
and the randy archaeologists
precede me: it can be Hamilcar
or Horace's farm or the Last Stand
at Syracuse, I don't mind.
There are important nerves telling my
unimportant imagination
that the dirty sand is more
than a hatchery of cockroaches,
that a rotting pier is rich in injustice—
saddle the nightmares and let the driver
move off into the night;
I want to watch the Emperor's fish
in their pool at Baiae,
the exhausted hills, the horticultural bones,
the olives of death.
I've never been so depressed
as when I saw the Florentine
National Library on television,
and there are so many more books to come!
I shall write only a few of them,
but at the movement of timid breath
on the page this provincial passion,
this unreformed ignorance

will glow again
and the famous carriers of sadness
appear beside my writing hand.

STORY WHICH SHOULD HAVE HAPPENED

There should have been the Old Manse under creeper
with half a sermon lying on a desk,
the vague light reaching in to touch the roses—
  there should have been herb gardens and poppies.

Upstairs in the attic we should have found,
pressed in prizes, petals of bold wildflowers
and Uncle William's primus stove, initialled—
  there should have been picnics and smoke-smelling clothes.

The Monopoly Set should have dated from
just after the First War and the silver kitchen spoons
heavy enough to weight down a bag of kittens—
  there should have been afternoons sweet as verbena.

We should have known the pain of finding
goldfish floating bloated under lily leaves
and father with a burnt hand smoking wasps—
  there should have been hedgehogs in the tennis net.

The novels by P. C. Wren, though read, should soon
have yielded to the Brontës and Thackeray
and *The Ancient Mariner* with coloured illustrations—
  there should have been intimations of love and hate.

After closing the door the doctor should have whispered
what brought tears to father, while the tray
grew lighter carrying buttered toast and soft-boiled eggs—
  there should have been standards to measure death by.

We should have come back in manhood to
a new and vulgar family with a Rover outside
and the conservatory packed with magazines—
  there should have been paradise to be expelled from.

13

What should have happened happened to other children
in other places: I meet them, tall and fair,
at ease with psychoanalysts and women—
 there should have been fictions to be real in.

SEASIDE RESORT

With her nose turning from her shroud,
smelling of onion and Osborne,
the small black rained-on Queen
stares with disciplined eyes at the sea—
            between her and it
start and zebra-stop the export-worthy
cars, call the corpse-coloured gulls,
toe-tip and rock-a-nore the great
public and its implacable children.
            She can see fishing boats
and tankers, the only Imperial things
in her lawful eyes and even they
dribble tar like old incontinents
dripping it down their flies.
            She is more than a square—
she has all the Squares of England
and all the cats and hydrangeas at her call!
To be in two minds about her is right:
gone and for good riddance the Raj—
you ice-cream your mouth under her
undersized pedestal while the Eastbourne
Brass Ensemble showers its *Showboat*
Medley on the American-owned air,
but you regret Mr. Mendelssohn
and the plant collectors of Udaipur.
            The polemic here is death;
the old people are flaking away
beside the model village, the three-
hundred-foot embroidery and the eighteen
hole Miniature Golf Course.
The scorpions never move all day
in their glass case in the Zooquarium;
so many nuns come to the beach
to test their black against the wind

and in the rain the Marina drops
its yachting posture to look
like an abandoned Thirties Aerodrome.
          There will be stone on stone,
say the bells, whatever happens to trade,
and we have so much burying still to do—
you cannot withdraw from our
Christmas Club and its's not yet
time for the Resurrection.
          But try to be serious
like bombed-out Number Three of the terrace
and the bombazined Queen.
          In the hinterland,
important things like electrical farms
and literary shrines are showing up well;
further off still in London, the life of
statistics (while hiding from Germany
and Japan) is a big deal.
          But what can happen here?
A new Ice Cream Flavour or a boom
in Rabbit's Ears, the visit of a hundred
skinheads or a Television Team,
a Conference of Escapologists,
Christ walking on the water to claim
the record Channel Crossing?
          Nothing but the calm
of history dying, the beautiful
vulgarization of decay—
Empire gone, the pensioner
will ask for a single stick of gladiolus
in a laughing shop.
          I am almost in love
with the small black Queen in the wind
and I will not notice that the beach is full
of mussel shells and crab claws
and the smell is unimaginable

yet like your mother's corpse,
that the torn feather is a terrible
catastrophe, and I am cold
and lonely on an unimportant strand.

DREAM RESTAURANT

In this restaurant the flowers double-talk,
they have overheard our dates to die:
my side-plate is a schism of the moon.

Why is everybody leaving, elbowing aside
chafing dishes and napkin barbicans,
why has a nimbus ducked the world in blue?

These radical ends of thought: my liver
is excoriated from my back, I have hidden
my pain like valuables in a vase.

I must be firm on vulgar instances—
a bell ringing like spiteful rain at sea,
a photograph that bloodies my right hand,

Where we eat is the world, I didn't dream it:
my mouth is full of eucharist, forgive me
if I've swallowed the words for love.

They will come back, the pain comes back,
return of the native at dusk or dawn,
private, without flowers, sicking up his words.

Dark and dark, the inside of the dark.
I am the world's digestion, I am love,
I eat and am eaten perpetually.

was hungry, he said, which was why
'd come to this house, and the pink rose
npted him up the path—a dusky carmine
e his mother's old dress—immediately
'd noticed the knocker, Silenus's face,
ange for a modest country door,
d the eyes were polished bright in the dark
ass: he walked straight through the hall,
ghtly aware of cats and pictures,
l he met her, entirely naked, at
e kitchen door, humming *Va*,
nsiero and carrying a dish
strawberries

        Amalgam of gold and ice
        his hard ring colophoning
        her back as he pressed
        down on her: to carry
        back to Meredith Grove
        that adulterous sign
        was marvellous—she felt
        the breeze from round
        an avenue of urns, gardeners
        clipping at the back, this
        moment with a stranger,
        uproarious as brass,
        tender as vanity, making
        tomorrow that much
        less certain

                I am glad
                said the voice
                when you come
                to me; I
                show my face
                which my friends

say is nice,
but you can't
go back now
that you've seen
me. It means
nothing at all;
life must stop,
I want to
warn you, I
want you to
be happy!
Someone to talk to, slip the strap
round the small of her back,
watch the carbon sun in windows
set at regulo seven, soon to
be done to domestic brown,
a science of the heart to frame
with the childhood certificates.
Strangers now to all the tenses

even the chattering present,
met for a moment in a comic
schloss, for which at least
Ulysses and his dog felt some
gratitude; 'if it moves
make love to it, you may be
asked to die at its side.'
Once again he found himse
in that hall of whiskers and darkness—
how can you resent the familiarit
of hatstands? A woman who takes yo
into her may still love the wrong Verd
The maplewood door swung ope
at the broken ray of his drear
and he joined the gardeners loadin
turf on hexagons of lawn. Rook
boiled in a villeinage of trees

kicking a democratic stone, he tasted
self-love, licking off her salts:
the owners of the world had gone away.

BETWEEN TWO TEXTS

In you my lif, in you might for to save
Me fro disese of alle peines smerte;
And far now wel, min owen swete herte!
                    Le vostre T.

The scene is made, encarded on a play,
Our sunny afternoon, an Autumn's gift;
Eyes down in ransom, trembling fingers lay
On hers, knuckled with rings—we lift
The tone of hoping with a rush of words
(The consonances lie, the trembling thirds)—
After thirty, nothing really happens:
Programmes from the fire are lower lights
And if she lusts at all, it's self-defence,
The drawing-in of these and chronic nights.

Yet every gamey gesture tells a story—
The boozing is a boast, look at her glass,
She sips a little lying inventory,
The husband detail of a lambent farce
(Somewhere beyond the hell of restaurants
Our epic artist guilds his Hellesponts)
And double double lays you for the dark—
The girl you love is traffic for all myths
But you sit flabbergasted: *he'll* embark
At dawn and leave you with the million Smiths.

I'll take him up—he's heir to Gilgamesh,
The death worm from the nostrils softens him
And then he's made the Dragoman of Flesh—
The Innundator with the Morning Hymn
Storms to the tomb of the desert's conqueror
(His international speech an actor's blur),
An Eden comic strip that ends in green
Among the Crematorium flowers and tapes
of Solemn Melody—and I have been
Beside him showing suns to light his rapes.

This sound of anger is our childish urge,
The cluttered attic where the mind goes mad—
How well the spite of pain, the drunken splurge
Match confession: enlightenment is had
By saints and tyrants but by none so well
As lovers (we have entered them for Hell!)—
No afternoon is wasted if locked hands
Gesture alarm at premature burial
And Tolstoy waiting at the station stands
Lamenting the approach of Ariel.

Up at the Front, *nichts neues;* little's clear
Except the corpse shine and a broken sound
Located in the conscience of the ear—
Unhappiness is real as turning round,
It takes you to the grave (that Cressid-shed
Beneath the stones of Troy)—not to be dead
Consists in feeding life; feed hope like bees
With sweetness of survival, privilege
Of vanity and metamorphoses,
The crossing not the jumping from the bridge.

This said, I take the gift and smile on you
For suffrage of the afternoon. We're sexed
Like gods whose wishes never can come true
Unless the mortal part is burned—who's next
To feel the air's obsidian knife?
(Staying alive is now a way of life)
The Communicators' Charnel waits for us,
We have some pictures which will make them stare,
A marquetry of bones, a flame of dust—
Death is not peace but permanent despair.

Ek gret effect men write in place lite;
Th'entente is al, and nat the lettres space.
And fareth now wel, God have you in his grace!
                    La vostre C.

AFFAIR OF THE HEART

I have been having an affair
with a beautiful strawberry blonde.

At first she was willing to do anything,
she would suck and pump and keep on going.

She never tired me out and she flung
fireworks down the stairs to me.

What a girl I said over the telephone
as I worked her up to a red riot.

You are everywhere, you are the goddess
of tasells shining at my finger ends.

You set the alarm clock to remind us
to do it before leaving for the office.

You are classic like Roman gluttony,
priapic like St. Tropez' lights.

She put up with a lot: I forgot about her
and went on the booze—I didn't eat or ring.

I borrowed from her in indigence.
I was frightened and fell back on her.

An experienced friend told me in his flat
among the press cuttings: they've got to play the field!

Of course, I said, but I knew where that was—
down my left arm, my left side, my windy stomach.

She was sometimes late and when alone
hammered me on the bed springs like a bell.

She was greedy as a herring gull and screamed
when my dreams were of Arcadian fellating.

I woke in her sweat; I had to do something,
so called in Dr Rhinegold and his machine.

Meanwhile, the paradigm was obvious:
it's me that's in you said a polar couple—

me, the love of hopeless meetings, the odd biter;
no, me, the wife by the rotary drier

with the ready hand. Dr. Rhinegold moved
mountains for me and said the electric hearse

might not run. But you're sick, man, sick,
like the world itself waiting in Out Patients.

I know how the affair will end—
but not yet, Lord, not yet. It isn't hope,

it's being with her where the scenery's good,
going to concerts with her, eating Stravinsky.

It's something more. I haven't finished explaining
why I won't write my autobiography.

These poems are my reason. She knows
she can't leave me when the act's improving.

She could imagine our old age: a black-
fronted house in a Victorian Terrace

or a cat-piss Square. Working on Modernism
while the stark grey thistles push to the door.

She can't let me go with my meannesses intact,
I'll write her such letters she'll think it's

Flann O'Brien trapped in a windmill. I'll
say her the tropes of tenebrae (or Tannochbrae).

I'll squeal in fear at her feet—O, stay with me
I'll plead—look, the twentieth century

is darkening like a window; love is toneless
on the telephone with someone else to see—

only memory is like your tunnelling tongue,
only your fingers tinkering tell me I'm alive.

And took up his pen, the pale Misanthropos,
  His Chloe's shutter speeds and apertures
  Become obscene Pindaric like McClure's—
'O Gobble Gloria, O Descant on the Cross!'

Cold Ironist tradition! William Wordsworth,
  Straight and plain as any stumbling sheep,
  Saw right in and what he saw was deep
And he grew fleecy and his hooves struck earth.

Great Plainness, yes, but I am different,
  I have not heard of any natural style.
  Those are my crooked teeth and not my smile,
I have to make what should be Heaven-sent.

Item: Chloe is with the Castlemaines,
  The pornographic sun's parameters
  Tickle her orphaned genitals; she stirs
In sleep, she shakes the goddess' silver chains.

In point of fact, she's trawling in the park
  And Fenwick's dresses get her randy stares.
  I dare what any man etcet., who dares
Do more is none. Then soon the central dark.

Meanwhile, a schoolmaster is heard
  Praising the egotistical sublime
  And I demur. We live, I fear, in time
And death is a big thing and bigger word.

But I'll obey and join the school for love,
  So forthright Chloe who knows everyone
  Must serve my modern poems as their sun
And camera-like we'll all the pleasures prove.

ON THE TRAIN BETWEEN
WELLINGTON AND SHREWSBURY

The process starts—
on the rails pigs' blood,
lambs' blood in the trees

With a red tail
through the slab-white sky
the blood bird flies

This man beside me
is offering friendly
sandwiches of speech:
he's slaughtered twenty pigs
this morning—
                    he takes away
the sins of the word

I can smell his jacket,
it's tripe coloured,
old tripe,
drained-out, veteran tripe
that has digested the world

I shut my eyes on
his lullaby of tripe
and the blood goes back to bed

(Someone's got to do it
and I'm grateful
and my neighbour's grateful
and we say so,
but thank God it's only
fourteen minutes to Shrewsbury)

Fourteen minutes to consider
the girl reading Scott Fitzgerald—
she has a red cashmere top
bright as a butcher's window

Shut out the sun and the cameras—
I want to talk to a doctor
about Circe's magic circle—
'you see, it was on the woman herself
the bristles sprang
and the truffle-hunting tongue'

What is it makes my penis
presentable?
hot blood—
enough of it, in the right place

With such red cheeks
my interlocutor from the abbatoirs
must have hypertension

On his knees he has
a lumpish parcel, well-knotted
with white string—
it makes all the difference
when you know it's really fresh

At one time our species
always had it fresh;
one time there were no cashmere tops
or butcher's shops

It consoles me that poems
bring nothing about,
it hurts me that poems
do so little

I was born after
man invented meat
and a shepherd invented poetry

At a time when there are only
fourteen killing minutes
between Wellington and Shrewsbury.

IN THE GIVING VEIN

The evidence, like the weather, is from
An inner storm; the poem, like every poem,
Will be merely a beginning, the daring work
For Venus's mirror, a heap of ashes,
Never to be finished though complete:
The mirror must be walked through
And the one of many million crosses
Borne—the pollen cloud dispersing, spruce
Sadists and armorial villains stand
Plausibly among scales and trumpets,
Violence and punctilio masked by falling
Almond blossom; then from the dream
A voice proclaims the flag and day of evil,
Indifferent to irony and liberal shame.

This is the gift I would refuse—I'd take
Well-water from a town of towers,
Make history of grey femurs and hot
Processions watched from reedy rivers:
The ingredients are myself, a nuisance
In a marmalade tomb grinning at
Centuries of cards, a savant with
A Cockney grammar interrupted as
The aristocratic plane drops, a storm
Of poets landing like Columbus' men
To bring back a pox to infect the twenty-six
Letters of the alphabet. There'll be no home
But that low-water amniotic
Whose sounds are caucus to the will to live.

No pressure on my chest and yet I'm not
In the giving vein. I have about me
Those moveables of eyes that dreams
Have sanctified. The weather is dull, no mist,

The lake is flowing in the wrong direction,
Early to work and the postman with
Words that fall down if they're leaned on.
Extraordinary that victory can be snatched
From such small things—a shift in
The weight of nouns, a new nickname
For God, a flower lasting an extra day—
We're in a fire, singing; I'm the one
Whose voice you can't hear; perhaps my round
O is agony, I shall insist it's praise.

A HINT FROM ARIOSTO

Hoisted on its great crane, the world laughs
As it goes upwards. One philosopher at least
Will picture in his hanging garden the yellow
Helmets and jackets of the hardworking gods;
It will take the rest of time to finish this
But thank Heavens the idea is working. Father
Helios is a bone merchant, yet we shall see
Life in the paper veil of a fontenelle. This
Is preambulum. It was the moon I wanted to tell
You about. American feet have walked on it
And Russian wheels trundled over it. Moon
Has no madness or even phosphate—it lowers
A lamp inside Mankind's memorial dark.

Erstwise it's all comic strip. Astolfo lands
The Hippogriff and signals back he's A-OK
To the warring lovers in the Marches. Negative,
Little Italy, with your Papal rages and your
Pretty learning. Touchdown is achieved
On a floating fairground. Beyond his unctuous
Steed (who's grazing on some aldermanic grass)
He sees a lake of quite unblemished purity—
All around, at every point, historical egos
Silver their reflected lips; the willing air
Is squandered on waves of lovers' words,
Truthful to touch and grammar: I die,
They say, and live to die again. No world says no.

Not just lost contracts and lost looks are found:
Bigger things, like souls, come swimming in—
What you fished for in sly intimations, woke
With on the salt of mirrors, here is real estate.
Solid as Sandgate are the Gothic passions,
Youth's exaggerations, suicidal tearducts;

Murder's gas a puff of birthday talc; most
Notably the silver words are real—those poets
We call holy or phoney find their clauses ring;
A bit of theatre cracks in a round bell;
The word *darling* pulses ceaselessly,
Comes in from the rain to put its arms
Spontaneously round the warm recorded heart.

Can Astolfo take it? He writes a letter home—
'No, eternity's not boring and the sounds
Of love are even smoother than a Florentine's;
Kindness for constellation and not cancer—
That's something to write home about. Love
Requited makes a garden without sundial
And all the madness which fills up earth
Is playing croquet here. Yet, my Paladins,
I am harnessing the Hippogriff once more
And shall sail for the sun. Look up from Hell
Upon my comet: earth and moon are merely shapes
Of the great plainness: you win a few, you lose
A few—only imagination is yourself.'

THE DUST

How many divisions has the dust
as it drifts upon the lukewarm land?

We have matched it with our treaties,
our helicopter shadows;
when it shifts formation
there will be lights on after midnight
in several hexagonal rooms.

Plural, it plays with the calm of men.

The mortal magnolia has it like moth's wings,
it's shaken out as salt from a tablecloth.

The Two were formed from this,
according to instructions
in the Scout Book on that first of campings out—
the cuscus looked and the slow worm sat
in a circle with itself: fasting, magnetism,
courage: they were our signs.

The Saviour of the State was accoutred
in his people's love, but a detachment of dust
rose from Spanish wheels.

Oh, but the dust, the gold-faced dust
from the Valley of Kings and Aunt Teresa's atomiser—
the aphids and the asteroids of change!

These are the priest's raised hands
and the lecturer's special slides
(for metropolitan audiences over thirty)—

As Doctor Danvers said—the cycle has one constant—
from the grub to the cyclone, the beta particle
to Donatello's chisel, the incorruptible body
to the pains of Hell—
only this milky dust.

Only dust the worm loved
singing at the river's mouth,
dust in the church of little spines,
dust where the library was burned.

Such clever men to start at starlight
when the dust lies low.

To know that when we land
the dust will be waiting.

Just as now a turn of wrist has sent a jot
of it over the rail to April.

Clear like a beast's old eyes
or Aphrodite's sweat-drops:

To please the dust by dying,
dying and returning—

To be worthy of the knowledge
that dust is only windows—

Not like the frightened Wit, brushing himself
ceaselessly behind sealed doors,

Nor the space in the crystal
where dust can never gather,

To live the while we live
just in this word, a dust.

AT SCAVANGER HOUSE

We're here today by courtesy of Mr. Eye—
    forever and forever, with the lint,
    the bathing box, and eighteen Centigrade.

Nobody may leave the building until
    the larder and the lavatories are searched,
    comments to be *sotto voce*.

While you're waiting, a tape of a run-over cat
    will be played,
a German Interviewer is approaching
    at 33,000 feet.

They'll tell you its's rehabilitation of the senses,
    all are to be sent to dig irrigation ditches,
we have rejigged the major scales and Bannockburn.

If it were possible to be with the Skalds
and have heroic syntax, that would be well—
    watching the mast as the helm goes over,
    fish in the panel of a wave—
no, it's not possible, and neither is New York.

We shall prove to you that blue is not a colour.

We defy you to say that this is just a dream.

By courtesy of Lichfield, migraine has hit Europe,
    trains at Rohrau are turning back,
    grease wanted for the guillotine.

Make it new! This afternoon you can choose
    between *Malleus Maleficarum*,
The Scratch Orchestra, and *Persuasion on Swings*.

Correction, there is also a Ballet Concrète
entitled *Pluralism, Compassion and Social Hope.*

I was under a yew tree in a churchyard
     when a poem crawled on to my collar:
it's in a bottle for the children;
we must find out what it eats,
     God will be pleased.

Calling Mr. Ear, there is a call for Mr. Ear,
will Mr. Ear come to the Front Desk please?
News from the Moon, an opal outcrop of tears,
     Unrepeatable (suggestions?) (bargains?)

And Judges job, and Bishops bite the town,
And mighty Dukes pack cards for half a crown.

Now melancholy walks the mossy Grange,
quiet and birds contend in multiple leaves
beside the White Garden and the piled-up banks
of rhododendrons—
               the stars are thinking
thoughts which may be mercantile
                 so grave a night
for loving and repairing love.

'The muscles of the under-dead are stirring,
rippling like roots that lift the concrete path,
straying from the house to track the goldfish
who rise to question Kipling's outheld hand,
then scatter to seek fantails of the dark . . .'

Something has been found below the elms,
     it's on the billiard table—
please call for Mr. Nose, will Mr. Nose report
     to the Matron immediately!

We need his expert knowledge,
we think this soft and jellied thing is death.

Oh, Mr. Eye, Mr. Ear, and Mr. Nose,
we'd like to introduce you to Mr. Mouth
who takes all things into him.

He's the owner of the house, his family
has all fishing rights, his books
are rarer than Monckton Milne's—
when you get to know him you'll agree
living and dying are his business.
A toast to Mr. Mouth, the good and bad,
our benefactor, Mr. Mouth. Last Georgian,
Last Aristocrat, he shuns the demotic
vagina but he'd lend his toothbrush
to a friend. A true soul, Mr. Mouth.

And, as in Peacock, they went on talking through the night
    till the postman brought
   sun and thunder to the door—

The goldfish woke for another hundred years
    and a tip of ivy reached
the highest brick on the sunless North Facade.

THE KING OF LIMERICK'S ARMY

On the left flank a brigade of nettles
defying the corn-ingesting hens,
On the right, athwart the pig-yard,
squadrons of righteous cow parsley,
In the centre, unperturbed as Hannibal,
bracken already gold with epaulettes.

Serene, they flutter over the stone-cooped dead,
they bear American Researchers shoulder-high—
Aspirants to Namesakes are pageing Synge
among memorials to a weird hunger:
Yes, these are oaks that Edmund Spenser saw
destined to ambush floats of pretty kings,
And the stirrups hang, the stirrups hang at ease
from horns of clay, from long prolonged pursuits.

Here fell the noblest, the brave O'Byrne,
strung to a side of bacon in his grief,
Rowing on swan water, the platitudinous priest
asked of the virgin death a little flower,
Upside down hung Hahessy for a bet,
three quarts of the stuff draining from his throat—
Nonpareils that had the magic in them
gone under the sincere soil with nothing done.

Grey paths the clouds make over everything,
a shadow corrupts and the thinking wind relents—
I was in service in the war of damp,
that was the famine year, the failure of the sap:
We export Crosses to the Bronx, our politicians
are plural as the grasshoppers in June,
The Universe is ending, a million thoughts at once
sealed in a collapsar till eternity.

We can face such concepts here, our army
has its rations, the weeds, the jokes, the softening air;
Down a black hole to tumble; well, the church
was there before us and Father Fogarty understands—
If it's a matter of years, the Lord has many,
and a field or two of Limerick besides.
Spacewards fan the radio waves, scientists
tingle like small boys with tadpole jars,
Ninety per cent of the Universe is dead
but our king's army is in acorn time
And blustering by the stream his powerless horde
undoes tomorrow what is fixed today.

THE GREAT COW JOURNEYS ON

Standing here where prophecy peers out
from breasts of rock, I see the turnpike
furies eat the flesh of soldiers killed
in battle—the Gate of Scythes, the Tank Upland—
next under bossy palms the Holidaymakers'
Hell, fused by speedboats and the halcyon
furnace: there the old pus of Europe weeps
for what was tears, the carpet of easy love
shrinks limbs to ricket shapes. Along the Gulf
of Time huddle the former empires, cold states
now peeling frontages for the tanned police—
some lost souls there still show the hero's
strutting jaw, the last heritage of his eye
in fallen witness. Along the Bastion
of Monorails, I see the future in a skin
of lights, the breathless people sacred to
the God of Fracture. Prometheans at ease
among the stolen fire, they filter the sun
through their transparent hats and
walk about with conferenciers' smiles.
Then the domain of Merely Magic, static
between the feeling creatures' nerves, these
odes of men in paper palaces outbalance
the engineering deities and are wise with awe.
My mind can go no further. At the foot
of a fetid lake the latest Herakles
rubs oil in his hair—as the stinking waters
fade, the hero rises up to new insanity—
a race of Titans without glory, pulse
of the future in their salt-packed fields,
they have no purpose but to start again.

DELPHI

There is a view of the sea through three tall trees;
We are not more than an hour from the best beaches
And the sun is so hot you might think a special
Lens hovered perpetually over our precincts.
Magistrates, families, and spinsters have learned
Extreme things here: pilgrims too have plodded
Past meaningless walls, the eye of a place-god
Watching from a piece of broken glass. NEVER
ASK . . . says a torn poster which doesn't intend
To be frightening—we have advertised the heart's
Wants since Aphrodite was a girl. You can have
A bathing hut and a packed lunch and if you speak
Quietly and take the occasional hand of cards
With the doyen of landladies she may utter through
Her muslin one of the aboriginal truths.
Our gardens are planted too late again
And the jittery clock at the Town Hall has forgotten
If Salamis or Mafeking was the time of its life.
The oldest resident, summing up sanctity and
The bracing air, says we have the seediest of
Perihelions, our tone of prophecy is due to
The prevalence of sunburn and the number of
Vegetarian restaurants. The many Conventions we have!
Addressed by bishops and conjurers—
The ladies with streaky hair who study gin
Through 2 p.m. light, the serene hum
Of vacuum cleaners always in another room,
The documentary film makers downing vodka
And lime, shouting how marvellous it is
In such a god-forsaken place! They are wrong,
We have never been abandoned: truth
And health are neighbours of death
And we know the home addresses of both;
Also we can make eternity seem like

44

Sunday afternoon. Our Kursaal and our
Public Gardens are haunted by butcher birds
And lovers' conversations—between us
And Olympus are plains of model dairies
And many unpolluted trout streams, yet a cloud
On the face of the gods will be clear to us
By breakfast, a shift in the balance of power
Exclaimed along the mole by frantic gulls.
What's worrying them in far-off Athens and Rome,
Where is the fleet becalmed, which hybridized
Plant will open up a hinterland? Ask by all means,
That and when your girl will learn to love you
And the weather and the trade figures. The statues
Of flayed Marsyas and the Generals of the Ashanti War,
Cross-pollination attributed to Hermes Trismegistus,
The Labours of Hercules in the *Arcana Arcanissima*,
Miss Austin's walking shoes—these and every notion
Will worry you in the Tower Museum. Our advice
Is to climb the hill to the giggling grotto
And hear the waves (just like cheese grating),
Take a good book (*The Childhood of Alexander
the Great*)—before dropping off, try alternately
Following squadrons of bees in the Corporation
Poppies and the shark fins of speedboats zizzing
Through the bay. Love? Money? Time?
Perish the thought! We assure you
There are no matters of importance left
And no questions worth asking. The clouds
Are parked in the fields. This is drowsy D. . . . i,
The happy haven, a good place to come to die.

TWO POEMS WITH FRENCH TITLES

Le Théâtre de bruit

Down they come from Valhalla,
the Noisy Ones with outsize noses
and phosphorescent breasts. The gold
piles up around their golden hair
(not one but has a numbered
account in a Swiss Bank): this
is going to cost someone a lot
of gravy. Be quiet in the Wings—
the other wings are beating; this
is nothing less than Apotheosis
and from the Burgtheater to
the Opéra Comique good sense
gets a beating. It's just as well
or how else could laurel help
a flying girl or the wonderful
skin of a diver bargain for
peace at last on the floor of earth.
The gods look after us well
but they're not exactly economical—
indeed no, Peer, but their faces
have the new wet look and one day
it may even pass for tears.

Mort aux chats

There will be no more cats.
Cats spread infection,
cats pollute the air,
cats consume seven times
their own weight in food a week,
cats were worshipped in

decadent societies (Egypt
and Ancient Rome), the Greeks
had no use for cats. Cats
sit down to pee (our scientists
have proved it.) The copulation
of cats is harrowing; they
are unbearably fond of the moon.
Perhaps they are all right in
their own country but their
traditions are alien to ours.
Cats smell, they can't help it,
you notice it going upstairs.
Cats watch too much television,
they can sleep through storms,
they stabbed us in the back
last time. There have never been
any great artists who were cats.
They don't deserve a capital C
except at the beginning of a sentence.
I blame my headache and my
plants dying on to cats.
Our district is full of them,
property values are falling.
When I dream of God I see
a Massacre of Cats. Why
should they insist on their own
language and religion, who
needs to purr to make his point?
Death to all cats! The Rule
of Dogs shall last a thousand years!

THE ISLE OF INK

Es gibt ein Reich wo alles rein ist ... Totenreich
Ariadne auf Naxos

The final purity is to have nothing to say.
   The portals of Carthage crack, burnt umber spills
Among the bees. Art is what should get you a lay.

They don't (the young don't) like these lazy frills—
   The approximations, *terza rima* (loose),
Garrulous on wine and priggish about pills.

Why sod about? Blood's running down the sluice,
   Napalm in the knickers, if I may quote Jeff.
We need a new art, with angles all obtuse.

Our Oxon. must be oxen, loveable, tone-deaf,
   And masters of *non sequitur*. Why not
Fold in bird music, too? Birds can't read a clef.

Joy the Holy Fool, the Bombed-up Buzzard—what
   Do we need with Dostoyevskys? Play
With the big boys till it pours and you get wet.

Alas, there's a kingdom among republics, where
   You have to dry your eyes and face the sun,
Someone's left you, why else would you be there?

But it's too bad each tear weighs a ton,
   Too bad the god is late, the ferry passes by;
Purity is gas or tablets or a gun.

Across the island before Friday's footprint's dry
   A crabby old creature's got his easel out
(Not his prick, he'll do that by and by)

And cursing critics, friends, the time, the doubt,
    The headache, heartbeat, hangover, *et al*,
He's painting Carthage from a shit-redoubt

All pocked and wattled—yes, he's Romantic, pal,
    But he's taken the path away from the abyss
Towards the line I took from Hofmannsthal:

His proper terrain, while he lives, is this,
    The highest pile-up which our bones will make,
A ten-tiered city or life lost with a kiss.

He's not tuned in to Cage, he's on the Lake
    With Virgil's sulphuretted dead; it's like
A pond, man, where a thing armed with a rake

Etcetera—a million toddlers ride the bike
    Of Hardly Art. The rest of us will stay
On the Isle of Ink, postmarked *Totenreich*.

CAN YOU CALL IT A VOCATION?

In an age of fashionable innocence
when careerism is the purest career,
to have ambitions of complexity
and yet lack patience entirely . . .

They have their hands on the levers
of definition, they are synchronizing
their watches by Basho's moon

To be unable to take ecology seriously
having polluted your own body
since childhood, including an island
of jettisoned trash called love . . .

They are playing games with new rules,
talking like foreign films, attending
Symposiums on the Great Leap Forward

Bothered by books like 'The Complete Wet Girl',
to try to get beyond all this fiddle
only to find it's concerned with rituals
of the braves and the bad-tempered bears . . .

They are taking the varnish off Shakespeare,
their oracles have pronounced: 'Anything too silly
to be said or sung can always be staged'

To dream of an Horatian present and wake
under a shower of bad odes written
by provincial sympathizers, the Festival
of Aniseed Balls having doubled its grant . . .

They huddle in a space of starlight
ignoring the clever L and his memo to
his countrymen on sausage and compendia

Baffled by our age's revival of the art
of otherwise, steaming for love, to hear
a hot tail say, 'I won't sit on your face, Frank,
I'm talking to this guy about Dante Alighieri' . . .

They have put the future on tape
and debate it while guns are raised
in wet provinces under a fanatic moon

THOMAS HARDY AT
WESTBOURNE PARK VILLAS

Not that I know where in this changed district
    He may have walked under unwarming sun
Through a hedged righteousness already bricked
Up to the pale sky and the many chimneys clouding it,
    Nor where black steeple, tar-gate, and gun-
bright anthracite held back the Spring and the exact green
                                to bring it.

Though the smoke's gone now, the old frailty shows
    In people coming unexpectedly out of doors
Hardly renumbered since his time: each house knows
As many stories as in the iron sublime we call
    Victorian. Suicide, lost love, despair are laws
of a visiting Nature raging against proof and practice and
                              changing all.

Here, rather than in death-filled Dorset, I see him,
    The watchful conspirator against the gods
Come to the capital of light on his own grim
Journey into darkness; the dazzle would tell
    Him these were the worst of possible odds—
ordinary gestures of time working on faces the watermark of
                              hell.

CHORUS AT THE END OF THE FIRST ACT

After the hours of singing and the long vowels
which ape the roundness of the heart
after the apprentice thunderclap
presaging the Ebony God
after the maidservants with plain needs
and coloratura of fingers in the dark
after the arias of determination, after the soap-clean light
and windows of first communion

Since the flute is stalled on the still plain
and towers can be seen a hundred miles
since the shattered jug is evidence
of complicity at the highest level
since the box is locked and the key in the river
and the mattress of fire is given to the guest
since the wolf's belly is filled with stones
and the pot of fat is hid in the rafters

Now the watchmen publish the hour of death
commending the citizens to love their wives
now the prophet is shown his face on a tray
and stone weeps and the blanket speaks
now the stout lovers are naked as naphtha
and watch is kept and is not kept
now the wound is fed, the betrayer enters
the city at the rising of the moon.

TENDING TOWARDS THE CONDITION

The news has reached the frogspawn,
our world is ransomed, spring rain
brings down a veil of weed, the Arno
the colour of Advocaat, another round
of tasks performed. To have nothing to say
fills large books with responsibilities—
as I said to the man in *Niccolino's*,
Do away with form and you drown
in the infinite chances, especially
as darkness and other persons' phlegm
puts such a strain on you. As I sit,
slightly drunk with change from a thousand lire,
I hear the pens of cataloguers circling
the evening: in this episode the ghosts
of Hoboken and Pincherle remind me
how much time there is in sixty years.
I will put out sugar for the scholars
and steal their honey—a sort of happiness
is tombed in the *Volta dei Mercanti*,
a breeze springs up and fluffs the sparrows,
another half carafe sets the moon sailing
or a blaze of rain to cool the customers—
there is a shape to the world, more real
than time, more absolute than music.

THE TOMB OF SCARLATTI

Average depth of graves, four feet—
the illusion of allegro in our light
is hard: that Iberian heartlessness
is still with us but not such sweetness.
What miracles for the twentieth century
among castrati, melons, and the dribbling kings!
Average length of sonata, four minutes, with repeats.

I hate the idea of Spain, yet for Domenico
I'd round each corner with its urine smell,
tickle the garden fish with a martyr's bone,
sit in the shadow of a cancered priest.
So many slaps of black! The old dust jumps
for American recordings, keyboard clatters
like cruel dominoes—E major fills the afternoon.

Santo Norberto gone: cat stalks complacent
pigeons. The old gods swim for home.
What are the conversions? Scholars' rules
and lace handkerchiefs become duennas' breasts
leaning from all top windows. A tourist bus
is draped with moonlight while the sounding notes
go past like carloads of the glittering dead.

LA DÉPLORATION SUR LA MORT
D'IGOR STRAVINSKY

1

From Colleoni's shadow
in a final purple,
out of the grinners' black,
an old man in a box
is carried to a gondola
and warped to the Isle
of the Dead: the cypress dark
must come to everyone
or the refining fire.
This is the death of Europe,
this is the eclipse—
an oar rises on the lagoon,
the flies rise from the camera-
man's breakfast. Pray
for all who have not known
such love and energy;
we are all guilty of dying,
we have gone under the trees
in the buzz of water,
expatriates of godsend
lamenting the machine
of genius and the Great Chute
of Twentieth-Century Death.

2

Plorans ploravit in nocte
But he was not a tearful man.
You must praise God with
a little art if you have any.
et lachrymae ejus in maxillis ejus.

Converte nos, Domine,
ad te, et convertemur.
God promised us prophets
who would not cry in an orchard,
the clockwork was all sinew
and Fabergé disintegrated
on the moon. 'Sunless
as a mushroom farm',
Los Angeles and death!
Innova dies nostros,
sicut a principio.

3
I've sugared all this verse to please Persephone
whose face is lacquered with her occidental tears;
she loves and praises in her petty underground
all those who do not shun the major modes.
Art is not religion, if death is—
one chord will carry us home: I bless the imps
of time who set his brain to ring before
self-murder got into aesthetics and the God
of Lyre-Strikers was known as Environment.
Praise to the end, an apotheosis by augmentation—
even the Georgics of Factory Farming have a place,
the new simplicities inherit complexity
to train against; we shall not talk of God
though Devils live; Marsyas' skin speaks for Civil Rights
but Apollo won't leave Heaven, his divine injustice
leans like a tall light among the cold immortals.

POSTCARD POEMS

*Orcagna—Detail from the fresco, The Last Judgement, The Inferno—
Santa Croce, Florence*

> Repentance comes too late. The camp fiends
> put on a fashion show. O wring your hands
> in eau-de-nil regret. Toasted with friends,
> the damned tiptoe on the burning sands.
> Orcagna, Florentine, your sexy smell
> is semen frying in the pans of Hell.

Sir Joshua Reynolds—Lady Mary Leslie—Iveagh Bequest, Kenwood

> Mary had a little lamb,
> four plump little lambs and a band
> of blue about her waist—
> insipid Mary was whey-faced,
> Daddy spent all day at the kennels,
> yet I praise this picture for the sake
> of once-fashionable Reynolds
> and to spite now-fashionable Blake.

*Domenico Veneziano—Profile Head of a Young Woman—Kaiser
Friedrich Museum, Berlin*

> Daddy's got the top interior decorators
> at the Palace. Mummy's the best-dressed
> woman in Tuscany. I met a poet
> with good manners, called Poliziano.
> It's hot today and the sky's hardly ever
> so blue as in this picture. I look
> as though I've got the collywobbles or
> I've swallowed a Latin Grammar:
> you'd never guess the things I can do
> with my lips. I'm seventeen and bored again.

Pisanello—La Principessa di Trebizonda—detail of fresco, Santa
    Anastasia, Verona

> I have dreamed of green bishops
> and almond-flavoured air,
> I have seen devils hi-jack
> the nimbus of a minor saint
> from an Ossuary by an Inland Sea—
> the Post is very bad, the wind
> is making tourbillons around my hat,
> it ruffles my cat Jesu, the four legs
> of impassioned platitude;
> from the depths of my calendar
> I send you two words—MUCH LOVE!

J. M. W. Turner—The Parting of Hero and Leander—National
    Gallery, London

> Love was always like this: a broken egg
> in the sky, dawn with its regulation
> Heartbreak and evening with a train to catch.
> The high buildings are not real, only the hopes.
> *Nous sommes aux mois d'amour.*
> Instead, the painter goes back in his eyes
> and the poet dreams he sees this incredible sky.
> Then the water breaks over his head. Praise
> on your birthday from the swimmer and his gods.

Peter Phillips—Random Illusion No.4—Tate Gallery

> Like the dove said, when you got
> a military-industrial complex going
> for you, you can blow rings round
> any old abstract scruple and have
> enough left over to endow the arts.
> Big nations have wingspan and it ain't
> Chrysler alone that mows down midgets.
> Now all you liberal poets, get off
> your blocks and come on hawkish!

Albrecht Altdorfer—Landscape with a Footbridge—National Gallery, London

> When the hermit heard about Nature
> he'd forgotten he'd been living off
> dung and berries for half a century.
> What a wonderful invention, he said,
> God has given Man a perfect frame,
> but I wouldn't cross that bridge
> into the picture for fear philosophers
> would devour me like wolves.

Richard Hamilton—Interior II—Tate Gallery

> The world is enormous, as the old
> lens-grinder knew, inhaling fine
> flour of death in his twilight room—
> the home fleet of the past dresses
> along my lifted arm and wherever
> the archons shift their weight
> a bruise of power shows. I am
> becoming perfect in a room,
> salvationist veal, nearer
> the heart of truth, the wholly
> responsive, appropriate number.

Piero di Cosimo—detail from The Fight between the Lapiths and Centaurs—National Gallery, London

> The Race Relations Board should issue this
> as their Christmas Card. Just for a paradox—
> since even here nature and gentleness connive.
> Vanity and monsters will abort, classic certainty
> is mere placenta. Mid-picture, a cormorant
> or some such dive-bombs the sea. Let them
> rend and bite and bash, Darwinian heroes
> are hiding in the bush. All shall be well,
> the monsters end up on a frieze
> with genocide on rollers at the farm.

Masolino—Adam and Eve—detail from fresco in the Church of the Carmines, Florence

Only the snake's erect—
the man's planning to ask his secretary out,
the woman wants a refrigerator—
a frightful row is brewing:
Prometheus on the Rocks
or The Wreck of the Deutschland—
thank god for a good chair and a view
of pollution on the box.

Giotto—Portrait of Dante—Bargello, Florence

This serious young face, so like a Kennedy's,
poet and plenipotentiary and always
a citizen of Florence. Forgive them their books
and treatises and universities—not many poets,
even horrible Goethe, have argued a whole
town over to the true wing of the Guelphs.
I've eaten in a restuarant named for you
and seen your posthumous life-mask. You tell us
we never get home but are buried in eternal exile.

Pinturicchio—La Storia della Fortuna—Mosaic, Siena Cathedral

I cannot work out this allegory
of men and women on a crumbling cliff:
bare breasts with a sail, one foot on a globe
and one on a boat—no one seems worried
and the detail is very beautiful.
I'm writing this with experimental music playing
and suddenly I see how all art is aggression—
behind the brotherhood of man
creatures with shears spit and wait.